The Bushfire Babies

Written and illustrated by
Debra O'Halloran

Published by Boolarong Press,
655 Toohey Road
Salisbury Qld 4107
Australia.
www.boolarongpress.com.au

First published 2016

Cataloguing-in-Publication entry available at the National Library of Australia

Creator: O'Halloran, Debra, author.

Title: The bushfire babies / Debra O'Halloran.

ISBN: 9781925522150 (paperback)

Target Audience: For primary school age.

Subjects: Wildfires--Juvenile fiction.
Children--Juvenile fiction.
Children's stories.

Dewey Number: A823.4

Printed and bound by Watson Ferguson & Company, Salisbury, Australia

A bushfire rages through the bush leaving four babies to fend for themselves.

The four frightened bush fire babies joined together to search for their families ...

FIRE! FIRE! FIRE!

This fire began as a small spark from a careless person disregarding the warning signs. Out of control the fire burns, dancing on the surface of trees eating away the wood below leaving it black when it has had its fill.

Fire fighters work all night to keep the fire under control. The night brings a cool breeze and moist air which helps to dampen the flames.

As the sun rises the next morning the animals that survive slowly creep out of their hiding places.

One such survivor is baby Echidna who crawls out of his hole in the ground. He looks around and sees the ground is covered in white ash and the tree's turned black.

His mum had dug a hole and told him to stay there until the fire had gone. He searches for her but he cannot see his mum *anywhere*!

He waddles on, maybe his mum is near that tree, the Echidna thought to himself.

He hears something scratching at the base of the tree and calls out "Mum is that you?"

The young Echidna waddled closer to the tree. There at the base was a hole and in this hole popped out a head with two very bright eyes. It was Baby Possum, she gave a squeal and popped back into the trunk of the tree.

Echidna said "Hello Baby Possum, it is safe to come out now, the fire has gone." The Baby Possum stuck out her pink nose and sniffed the air. She looked at Echidna and said in a timid voice "Do you know where I can find my mum?"

Echidna replied "No I don't, I am looking for my mum too. We can look together ok?"

"Ok Er-e-Ekki!" said Baby Possum who had a little trouble saying Echidna so she called him Ekki for short.

Echidna and Baby Possum walked down the hill each calling out "Mum, mum where are you?" There was no reply.

"Ekki, I am so scared, what if we don't find our mums, who is going to look after us?" Said a very sad Baby Possum.

"We will be alright Baby Possum" Echidna said "Let's see if we can find some food here, I am a bit hungry."

Echidna stuck his nose in a log looking for ants while Baby Possum found a bush to climb up. She wondered what tasty morsels she will find in the branches when suddenly the bush began to move and bend and a terrible sound came from above.

"Eeek!" cried Baby Possum. She jumped clear of the moving bush and hid behind Ekki. "W-w-what is it?" said Baby Possum.

Echidna and Baby Possum looked at the funny creature who had long tall legs and a neck that seemed to stretch high into the sky. "Who are you?" asked Echidna.

The creature bent down low so that she could see the two friends on the ground. "I am Emu, who are you?" said the Emu chick.

Echidna told Emu who they were and how they came here searching for their mothers.

Folding her legs under her Emu sat down near Echidna and Baby Possum. She told them that her mother, sister and brothers were looking for shelter when Emu became separated from her family. She found a cave and hid there until the fire had passed and now she does not know where her family has gone.

Baby Possum went to Emu and climbed upon her back and hugged her long neck and said “It’s alright Emu, you can come with us to look for your mummy too! We will help you, won’t we Ekki?”

“Yes” said Echidna “We will help you look for your family too Emu.”

Together the three Bush Babies looked high and low further down the hill searching every possible log and tree.

It was not long before they heard a sobbing noise. The friends found a little brown wallaby crying in his hands. With a sniff and a hiccup the wallaby looked out at the new arrivals.

The little wallaby told the friends how he became lost. "I fell out of my Mama's pouch while we were hopping away from the fire. I was so scared, all the animals were running in all directions and I lost my mummy. I don't know how I got here."

Oh, poor Wallaby, you will be fine now cause you have us to look after you," said Baby Possum.

"We are looking for our mummies too, so you can come with us and we will look together," said Emu.

The four friends wandered for a very long time. When it became dark they found some where safe in a cave to huddle together and try to sleep. It was not a very restful night because they were so hungry and thirsty. The fire had burnt so much of their food that they could not find anything to eat.

The next morning they came to a high cliff edge and looked down at the bush. This made them sad, how were they going to find food and water or their families in this burnt out bush?

They walked on and on getting hungrier and more desperate for water. With heads hung low they struggled to make each step.

The group did not realise that they had come to a dirt road and had been following the bends this way and that way.

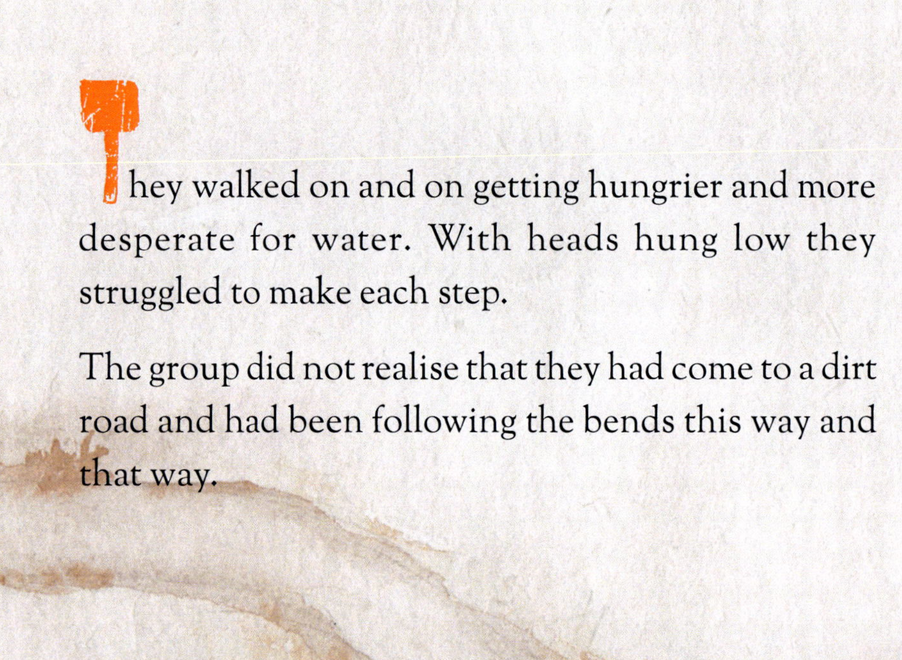

Something made them stop. They could smell water. Was it their imaginations? No it was not because they were drinking it and it felt so good going down their dry throats. It was wonderful.

Feeling a little better Emu looked around. What was this creature? Emu had never in her short life seen anything like it.

Echidna said that it was a human. "They live on the other side of the hill and don't often come to the bush. Animals mostly hide when they are around as some are not nice, but my mum said there are some good ones."

The human poured more of the water into a dish on the ground. They lapped up the water which made them feel so much better.

The human spoke to the frightened animals and one by one gently placed them in cages. Baby Possum was scared, "What is happening Ekki?

"I don't know Baby Possum, we will have to wait to find out." Echidna said to her.

It was dark except for the light coming from one corner under the tarp. The vehicle began to move and the cages bounced up and down. All they could do was hang on and wait for a chance to escape. At least they are together.

The humming noise and the rocking of the vehicle eventually settled them and they began to drift off to sleep.

The truck hit a bump in the road! The cages in the back rattled and shook. The four friends woke with a start and looked around making sure they were still together.

Where are we Ekki?" asked Baby Possum.

"I don't know, I fell asleep" said Echidna. "Me too" said Emu and Wallaby together. They looked out through the gap in the corner and what they saw was exciting.

Suddenly the vehicle stopped and the cover was tossed off of the cages. The four friends became frightened.

The man said soothingly to the friends "It's alright little ones you will find plenty of food to eat and fresh water to drink here." They did not understand what the man said but they felt that this man meant them no harm.

Lifting the cages the man put them on the ground and opened the cage doors one by one. Emu and Wallaby jumped out and waited for Baby Possum and Echidna.

Baby Possum, when she was released, went straight to Echidna's cage and waited for the man to open the door of his cage.

Together again they looked around in astonishment. In the valley below the grass was thick and green. The tree branches were covered in leaves and near the water's edge are all kinds of animals and birds.

All of a sudden Emu shouts out "Mum, mum, I'm here!" she looked at the others and said "There's my mum, down there!"

"Yeah! That means our mum could be down there too!" said Wallaby. "Let's go and have a look." Together they scampered down into the valley in search of their mothers.

One by one they each found their mothers. They were so happy to be together again with their families that all the animals cheered.

That night they celebrated late into the night.

As the years go by the four friends have grown up and had babies of their own who also play and live happily together.